Journaling Through

ANCHORS
for the
SOUL

A Guide to **Help Individuals Process** *Loss and Grief*

JOHN MARK HICKS

An imprint of Harrington Interactive Media

Journaling Through Anchors for the Soul: A Guide to Help Individuals Process Loss and Grief
Copyright © 2019 John Mark Hicks

Requests for information should be sent via e-mail to HIM Publications. Visit www.himpublications.com for contact information.

ISBN 978-1-970102-24-6 (Print)
ISBN 978-1-970102-25-3 (Kindle)
ISBN 978-1-970102-26-0 (ePub)

Cover and interior design: Harrington Interactive Media
www.harringtoninteractive.com

Printed in the United States of America

Contents

Getting Started

How to Use This Journal

Journaling is a journey. We begin in one place and, by the grace of God, we find ourselves further down the road.

There are no guarantees, of course. Grieving is not a mechanical process by which we make positive progress as if putting together a piece of furniture. Nothing in this guide ensures healing.

Grief is a dark place. It feels like we are trapped by an enemy, and we have little hope, perhaps no hope, of liberation. It's difficult to concentrate, to see the goodness that surrounds us, and sorrow is constantly by our side. Tears flow so easily, and we feel like there is no end to them. Grief blinds us, burdens us, and zaps our energy.

In my own life, I tried to stuff it, ignore it, and avoid it. I lived in a dark place and pretended I was in the light. But the darkness suffocated any authentic joy, and I functioned more like a zombie—alive but lifeless. In my avoidance, the hurt came out sideways in negative ways, and I deepened my wounds rather than finding healing.

Somewhere along the way, someone shared a metaphor with me that helped me. Let me share that metaphor with you: While we rightly find ourselves sitting in the darkness for a time, there comes a moment when we begin to move through the darkness toward the light. We can wait for the light to dawn, but perhaps it is better to move toward the light. It's like living in a dark tunnel, and as long as we remain where we are, the darkness will continue to oppress us. At some point, through the help of friends, community, and faith, we begin to move toward the light and, by the grace of God, we will begin to see some light at the end of the tunnel, though the darkness remains with us.

This is why processing grief is important. Journaling opens us up to our own feelings in the presence of God and gives the Holy Spirit opportunity to work in our hearts and emotions. By journaling, we engage Scripture, prayer, and our own hearts. We face our grief in the presence of God.

I offer this brief guide as a way of processing grief and loss while you read *Anchors for the Soul*. There are many ways to process grief, and I hope this will provide some helpful guidance.

Each journal entry is connected to a specific chapter in *Anchors for the Soul*. The entries begin with a biblical text, ask questions, and then propose an action. It may work for you something like this:

Step 1. Begin by reading the correlating chapter in *Anchors for the Soul*.

Step 2. Inside this journal, read and meditate on the biblical text provided for the entry:

- Read it out loud, or listen to someone read it. Sit in silence with the reading for a moment (perhaps 2–3 minutes).
- Read the biblical text out loud again. Identify some key phrases that you found meaningful. Write them down along with why they were significant to you.
- Read it out loud once more and write an observation about God and one about people.

Step 3. Respond to the questions for the entry by writing them down in the space provided here in this journal. Don't feel the need to answer every single question, but use the questions as prompts to help you journal as you see fit.

Step 4. Go back and read your responses and add a further reflection on how this exercise opened any new dimensions for you.

Step 5. Lastly, act. Reflect on and then respond to the suggestion at the end of your entry by doing something. For each entry, we offer an option for action.

I hope this is helpful. Progress in grief is difficult, and we are usually taking two steps forward and one step back throughout the whole journey; sometimes, it is one step forward and two steps back.

Use this resource in whatever way you think might benefit you. And all along the way, remember God's desire for you, as expressed in Paul's prayer in Romans 15:13 (NRSV):

> May the God of hope fill you with all joy and peace in believing,
> so that you may abound in hope by the power of the Holy Spirit.

Our Stories

Everyone's story is different, and everyone's suffering is unique. No one's story serves as a paradigm for everybody else. This is true of Job, the psalmists, and myself, as well as you.

At the same time, when we listen to another's story, we open ourselves to learning about ourselves and about our journey into the life of God. In Psalm 119 we hear the story of an ancient worshipper of God. This is not exactly your story or mine, but let us hear this Word to God about God in the presence of God.

First reading. Read Psalm 119:65-88 out loud and meditate on this passage.

Second reading. Read the passage again and write down key phrases you found meaningful.

_____   _____

_____   _____

_____   _____

Why did you find those phrases meaningful?

_____

_____

_____

_____

_____

_____

_____

Third reading. Read the passage once more and list one thing it says about God and one thing it says about people.

<u>God</u>   <u>People</u>

What is one way this passage invites you to participate in God's story?

_____

_____

_____

_____

_____

_____

_____

_____

_____

_____

_____

_____

_____

↝ Reflect and Journal

- Do you see the elements of lament in this section of the Psalms? What questions does the psalmist ask God?
- How is it "good" that the psalmist was afflicted? What did the psalmist learn?
- Where does the psalmist ultimately find comfort? Then, for what does the psalmist ask?

_____

_____

_____

_____

_____

_____

_____

_____

_____

_____

_____

_____

→ACT

Consider how God can give "songs in the night" and how God may have given you one or more of such songs. With whom can you share a "song in the night" that God gave you in the midst of your suffering? If you have one, share it with someone this week.

_____

BE ENCOURAGED

"When will you comfort me?" That question haunts many of us. At the same time, we appeal to God's steadfast love. We wait, and we groan. And as we begin the journey through our grief into the heart of God, allow yourself to sit with this difficult question without feeling the need to hear an immediate answer.

God Loves

It seems ungodly to doubt the love of God, but believers—in the Bible and throughout history—have doubted God's love. I have doubted it . . . often. Such doubt doesn't undermine faith, but it does energize our search for God's love in the midst of our pain. God's response to these doubts is Jesus. Simple, yes—but profound.

First reading. Read Romans 8:31-39 out loud and meditate on this passage.

Second reading. Read the passage again and write down key phrases you found meaningful.

Why did you find those phrases meaningful?

Third reading. Read the passage once more and list one thing it says about God and one thing it says about people.

<u>God</u>   <u>People</u>

What is one way this passage invites you to participate in God's story?

_____

_____

_____

_____

_____

_____

_____

_____

_____

_____

_____

_____

_____

_____

→ Reflect and Journal

- Notice the questions that appear in Romans 8:31-39. Write them down.
- How does Paul answer these questions? What is his evidence for these answers? How does he know?
- What are diverse experiences in Romans 8:31-39 that threaten our sense of God's love in our lives? How have you experienced some of these?
- Where, in your experience, has God demonstrated faithful love?

⇴ ACT

Read Psalm 136. You will notice how Psalm 136 affirms the steadfast love of the Lord after every praise or thanksgiving.

In the light of Romans 8:31-38, add lines that tell the story of God's love demonstrated in Jesus. For example, "God did not spare God's own son" followed by the line about the steadfast love of the Lord. Add six to ten lines to Psalm 136 below based on your understanding of Romans 8:31-38. Also, write a prayer of thanksgiving for God's love and the ways you have seen it in your life and faith journey.

A prayer of thanksgiving:

Make a gratitude list for the good things in your life. List at least 30! You can begin small ("I have indoor plumbing"), if you like. Think of 30 and write them down.

1.

2.

3.

4.

5.

6.

7.

8.

9.

10.

11.

12.

13.

14.

15.

16.

17.

18.

19.

20.

21.

22.

23.

24.

25.

26.

27.

28. _____

29. _____

30. _____

_____

_____

_____

_____

_____

_____

_____

_____

_____

_____

_____

_____

_____

_____

Pray through your gratitude list, giving thanks for each item. Simply name them and say, "Thank you, God!"

BE ENCOURAGED

At the cross, God assures us, "I love you." Though our tragedies and wounds may turn our hearts to doubt, God comes to us in Jesus and says, "I love you."

~

God Listens

Sometimes it seems like no one is listening. As we weep and groan, we feel so alone. We want to yell, shout, cry, and curl up into the fetal position.

God is listening. God gives us permission to yell and shout, to voice our doubts and questions, and to sit in our pain before God's face. Like David, we can pour out our complaints to God without fear of condemnation from God (Psalm 142:2).

First reading. Read Psalm 77 out loud and meditate on this passage.

Second reading. Read the passage again and write down key phrases you found meaningful.

_____   _____

_____   _____

_____   _____

Why did you find those phrases meaningful?

_____

_____

_____

_____

_____

_____

_____

_____

Third reading. Read the passage once more and list one thing it says about God and one thing it says about people.

<u>God</u>   <u>People</u>

What is one way this passage invites you to participate in God's story?

_____

_____

_____

_____

_____

_____

_____

_____

_____

_____

_____

_____

_____

_____

⇥ Reflect and Journal

- When have you experienced such pain that you were "too troubled to speak"? When have you experienced an inability to sleep?
- How do you think God heard the psalmist's prayer? In your imagination, at what point would God say to the psalmist, "This is too much," or "That crosses the line"?
- How does the psalmist move through the pain?
- Upon what does the psalmist meditate? To what does the psalmist appeal? What does the psalmist remember?
- Where does the Psalmist see God in the pain and in the life of the people of God?

→ᴊ Aᴄᴛ

Write Psalm 77:7-10 longhand three times. Read it out loud slowly over and over again for five minutes.

Psalm 77:7-10

Psalm 77:7-10

Psalm 77:7-10

Add your own complaints or questions (or both) to the psalmist's words. Write down at least five questions or complaints you have for God. Pray them!

_____

_____

_____

_____

_____

_____

_____

_____

_____

_____

_____

_____

_____

_____

_____

_____

Find a friend or a group to read Psalm 77 with you. Follow the reading exercise with the group—that is, answer the questions from the beginning of this session about what Psalm 77 says about God, humanity, and our participation in the story of God. Share your questions and complaints with them. Ask them to pray them with you.

BE ENCOURAGED

Sometimes believers feel uncomfortable voicing their complaints before God, and sometimes not. Perhaps a certain discomfort is healthy, but it is healthier to share honestly with our God. God loves us, and therefore we voice our hurts, doubts, questions, and complaints.

God Understands

No one understands! In a sense, this is true: each of our experiences is unique. Yet, suffering is something we also share with others. So, in another sense, others—fellow sufferers—actually do understand.

And God understands because God shares our suffering too! God became flesh, and through that flesh suffered *with* us, as well as *for* us. God knows suffering, so God understands our suffering. God knows us more than we know ourselves, and God in the flesh has experienced our suffering in ways more profound than we could ever understand. God knows, and God understands.

First reading. Read Hebrews 4:14-16 out loud and meditate on this passage.

Second reading. Read the passage again and write down key phrases you found meaningful.

....

....

....

Why did you find those phrases meaningful?

....

....

....

....

....

....

Third reading. Read the passage once more and list one thing it says about God and one thing it says about people.

God	People

What is one way this passage invites you to participate in God's story?

_____

_____

_____

_____

_____

_____

_____

_____

_____

_____

_____

_____

_____

⇀ REFLECT AND JOURNAL

- Consider how God became one of us. How does this change our understanding of who God is when we confess God became human, and how does this change how we perceive God, who is often envisioned as so distant from us?
- What does God's empathy say about the depth of God's love? Would you join another in their suffering just to share in it with them? What would it take for you to do so?
- What comfort does God offer through this empathy? How does the fact that "God understands" affect your experience of suffering?

→Act

Think of a life circumstance of someone you've watched from the outside but later experienced firsthand. For example, perhaps you have never been fired from a job, but you have known others who have. But now you yourself have been dismissed from a job. How did your experience change your perspective? Write down, in as many ways as you can, the difference between knowing about an experience and actually participating in it. Make your list at least five items, and remember to write how identifying this difference—the difference between knowing about something and experiencing something—changed your perspective.

Pray. Give thanks for God's empathy. Meditate. How does God's empathy empower your own empathy for others? Write down three ways your own suffering has given you more empathy for others.

BE ENCOURAGED

God understands. We understand, but God understands more deeply and more profoundly than we do. Whatever we feel in the midst of our suffering, God has felt it as well. You are not alone!

God Reigns

Really? God reigns? Then why am I in such pain? We know God loves us in Jesus. God listens to our complaints. God understands our hurts. But we wonder what God is going to do about it, and what God is really up to.

This is a difficult confession to make: God reigns. God is at work in our suffering, and the reign of God means that God will affect God's own purposes for us. But sufferers doubt this, and understandably so. Faith trusts God's love and hopes in God's purposes.

First reading. Read Romans 8:26-30 out loud and meditate on this passage.

Second reading. Read the passage again and write down key phrases you found meaningful.

_____   _____

_____   _____

_____   _____

Why did you find those phrases meaningful?

_____

_____

_____

_____

_____

_____

_____

_____

Third reading. Read the passage once more and list one thing it says about God and one thing it says about people.

God   People

What is one way this passage invites you to participate in God's story?

_____

_____

_____

_____

_____

_____

_____

_____

_____

_____

_____

_____

_____

_____

→ REFLECT AND JOURNAL

- According to Romans 8:26-30, what is God's goal for us?
- In what ways do God, Jesus, and the Spirit help us in seeking that goal?
- Where do you see God active in your life to move you toward that goal?

→ ACT

List your experiences of suffering in the first column below. In the second column make a gratitude list. The gratitude items do not have to parallel or correspond to the moments of suffering but are simply a list of gifts from God for which you are thankful. Then, in the third column, identify concurrent goods which arise as collateral beauty, even though your suffering is horrendous. For example, a possible concurrent good that arises from suffering could be new friendships, new community, or deeper community.

Suffering	Gratitude	Concurrent Goods

Suffering	Gratitude	Concurrent Goods

Optional: I recommend you watch the movie *Collateral Beauty*, which features Will Smith. It may help your eyes to see collateral beauty in your suffering.

BE ENCOURAGED

Collateral beauty is difficult to see, and it may be hidden from you for years. It does not minimize your pain. It does, however, provide insight, and it reminds us that God is still at work, even in our suffering.

God Wins

Our Christian hope is the resurrection of the dead in a new heaven and new earth. Because God raised Jesus from the dead and defeated death, eternal life is our inheritance.

This inheritance is filled with renewal. God is making, and will make, all things new (Revelation 21:5, 7). God heals, God recreates, and God invites us to possess our inheritance. God wins, and so do we.

First reading. Read Revelation 7:9-17 out loud and meditate on this passage.

Second reading. Read the passage again and write down key phrases you found meaningful.

....

....

....

Why did you find those phrases meaningful?

_____

_____

_____

_____

_____

_____

_____

_____

Third reading. Read the passage once more and list one thing it says about God and one thing it says about people.

God	People

What is one way this passage invites you to participate in God's story?

_____

_____

_____

_____

_____

_____

_____

_____

_____

_____

_____

_____

→ REFLECT AND JOURNAL

- As you reflect on Revelation 7, what is your "tribulation"? What in this vision of the future provides comfort in your present tribulation?
- How do you invest the hope of the future in your present and painful reality? What does that look like for you? Do you have a ritual or a practice that reminds you of this hope?
- Imagine joining this chorus around the throne and singing with this multitude that can't be counted. Who is present in that crowd that you knew and have loved here on the earth but is now before the throne of God?

⇒ ACT

What are your rituals of grief? In the space below, identify what you can do to help yourself grieve or deal with loss. For example, I visit my son Joshua's grave on Easter morning. My wife, Jennifer, purchases an annual figurine to remember Leah. Or perhaps you have a ritual of silence and solitude, or listen to music, or follow a prayer ritual of some kind. How do you grieve? If you don't currently have a plan, what would you like to do to help yourself grieve?

On the next page, journal about how the meaning of the new heaven and new earth, the resurrection, and the return of Jesus affect you in your grief. How do you connect your grief and God's victorious future? What does this mean for you?

Then on the third page, imagine a ritual or practice you might incorporate into your grieving that connects you tangibly and in a concrete way with your hope.

What I do to help myself grieve or deal with loss:

How the meaning of the new heaven and new earth, the resurrection, and the return of Jesus affect me in my grief:

_____

_____

_____

_____

_____

_____

_____

_____

_____

_____

_____

_____

_____

_____

_____

_____

_____

_____

_____

_____

_____

_____

_____

A new ritual or practice I can incorporate into my grieving that connects me tangibly and in a concrete way with my hope:

BE ENCOURAGED

God does not simply win; God transforms, renews, and empowers new life. As hard as it is to believe now, our suffering pales in comparison to the glory God will reveal.

SESSION 7

~~~

The Courage of Silence

Silence can feel awkward and uncomfortable to potential comforters. But it is the most powerful balm available for healing. It doesn't seem like both should be true. Nevertheless, many have experienced comfort in the silent presence of friends.

As people who would comfort others, we must have the courage of silence, and with that courage, those who suffer learn to trust God's healing presence through the presence of silent friends.

First reading. Read Job 2:11-13; 13:5; 16:1-5; 42:1-6 out loud and meditate on these passages.

Second reading. Read these passages again and write down key phrases you found meaningful.

------------------------------   ------------------------------

------------------------------   ------------------------------

------------------------------   ------------------------------

Why did you find those phrases meaningful?

Third reading. Read the passages once more and list one thing they say about God and one thing they say about people.

God	People

What is one way these passages invite you to participate in God's story?

✒ REFLECT AND JOURNAL

- Why do we feel so awkward with silence? Why does silence feel so inadequate in the face of suffering?
- What wisdom do you see in silence?
- How have you experienced silence as helpful when people have been present with you in your own suffering?

→ ACT

In order to learn silence, we must practice silence. Talking is too easy. Silence gives God space to encounter us without the distractions and the busyness of life. "Ponder it on your beds," the psalmist sings, "and be silent" (Psalm 4:4, NRSV).

Begin a practice of daily silence:

1. Start with two minutes, then three minutes, and keep adding minutes as you are able, until you reach ten minutes of silence. Acknowledge distractions that come and say, "I'll think about you later," and let them pass like leaves on a creek.
2. After your first time of silence, write down what happened: what you felt, what you sensed, what you noticed, or even how, perhaps, you heard God in those moments.
3. Finish by praying over what you experienced and ask God to come to you in future moments of silence.

In my first practice of silence . . .

I felt:

I sensed:

I noticed:

How I may have heard God:

_____
_____
_____
_____
_____
_____
_____
_____
_____
_____
_____
_____
_____
_____
_____
_____

BE ENCOURAGED

Silence. In the face of suffering, silence is our first, perhaps our best, response. Silence honors the pain rather than justifying it. Silence sympathizes with the hurting rather than explaining the hurt. Silence is the space in which God can do God's best work. Silence is where our humility and God's presence come together for healing.

~

A Time to Speak

There comes a time for us to speak. Silence is good as a first practice. At the same time, we are to share love and relationship through speech as well.

Speaking, however, is always about sharing one's own experience or expressing one's own feelings. We say, "I love you," rather than "you should . . . ." We speak in order to sympathize rather than to explain. We speak to comfort rather than to interpret.

First reading. Read Psalm 43 out loud and meditate on this passage.

Second reading. Read the passage again and write down key phrases you found meaningful.

_____   _____
_____   _____
_____   _____

Why did you find those phrases meaningful?

_____
_____
_____
_____
_____
_____
_____
_____
_____

Third reading. Read the passage once more and list one thing it says about God and one thing it says about people.

<u>God</u> | <u>People</u>

What is one way this passage invites you to participate in God's story?

_____

_____

_____

_____

_____

_____

_____

_____

_____

_____

_____

_____

_____

→ REFLECT AND JOURNAL

- Why do we want to know "why" we suffer? Should we encourage the why question? What value do you see in asking it?
- What words did people speak when they sat with you in order to provide comfort?
- What sort of words were comforting, and what sort were not comforting?
- How might the story of God, summarized in the five anchors, provide comfort when there is an opportunity to speak?

Act

Write in the space below (or sit down with a friend and share) the five anchors. Name them, explain them, and apply them to people in their suffering or to your own suffering.

Name one person you know who is suffering a great pain. Write out a prayer for them in the light of the five anchors. Share this prayer with the person when you think there is an appropriate time (if that comes).

A person who is suffering:

_____

My prayer for them:

_____

_____

_____

_____

_____

_____

_____

_____

_____

_____

BE ENCOURAGED

We share the five anchors when appropriate, and we share them in the light of our own experience rather than in how another "should" accept them. We share the gospel when we share the five anchors. We invite people into the story; we invite grievers to hear Good News. At the same time, we also sit with those who grieve, we weep with them, and we remain silent until God opens a space into which we may speak.

Moving Forward

How to Continue Living an Anchored Life

As we conclude this journaling experience, let me encourage you as you move forward. It's not easy to stay anchored. I wish I could say my life has always been anchored, and I wish I could tell you that my anchors will always remain words of comfort in my journey, instead of words of mystery and even doubt. Sometimes I feel unanchored. Healing from grief is like a rollercoaster ride. It has its moments of deep despair, as well as moments of joy and peace, and it keeps going.

To use a different metaphor, grief comes in waves. At the beginning, the waves are high and overwhelming. Throughout life—even thirty-nine years after Sheila's death and eighteen years after Joshua's—the waves keep coming. While they have never totally disappeared, the waves have slowed and shrunk. The journey of grief over any kind of loss is long and seemingly never-ending. Yet joy returns, renewal comes, and life continues.

There is no timeline for grief. There are no expectations that one should do "this" or do "that," or that *doing* something will be a cure or a healing balm. Every griever grieves at their own pace. At the same time, we need some pace at which we can move, even if it is taking baby steps. The five anchors have helped me keep pace.

How, then, do we stay anchored? Though everyone must find their path through loss (and it will look different for everyone), I have a few suggestions:

Continue to lament honestly. Tell God how you feel. If you have questions, ask them to God. If you are angry, voice it. If you have doubts or complaints, express them. Even if you don't think God is listening or you don't believe God is there, speak the pain out loud. It is a form of spiritual therapy, a kind of spiritual venting. Sometimes it is difficult to find the words to pray, and this is when I use the Psalms or other written prayers. Then, I don't have to find the words. Rather, those already-written words give me a voice with which to speak to God. Prayer is sometimes quite difficult in the midst of our grief, so let others pray for you and use their words as your own prayer language.

Find yourself in the story of Scripture. The Bible is neither a scientific nor a self-help book. It plots a story with God as the main actor. God calls us to participate in his story. When we read Scripture, God invites us to find ourselves there. When we locate ourselves within God's story, we are able to see the world through God's eyes.

Different episodes in the story resonate with different people. Some find themselves sitting on the ash heap with Job; some find themselves in the wilderness with Moses; and some find that their powerlessness is like Joseph in prison. Others speak the words of the Psalms or Jeremiah as their own, and still others recognize their pain in the weeping of Mary and Martha. The different episodes, however, are part of a single, grand narrative—the big story. This is a story of creation, brokenness, and hope. This narrative does not dismiss the pain but redeems it. The wounds are healed as God's creation is redeemed, and everything is made new. When we find ourselves in that story, we surrender to hope.

Engage your community. I used to think God and I were enough. My thought was that even if I had no one else, I would be fine because God can handle anything. But through my experiences, I learned that God did not make us like that. God created us for community. We do not flourish in isolation but in community. We need each other's help, and this is especially true when we suffer. Sufferers tend to isolate. Pain and shame do this to us, and it is exactly how shame wins: when we are alone, we die the death of our own self-pity, anger, shame, and worry. We destroy ourselves, as if a cancer is eating away at our soul. Community makes the difference for so many people. They find intimacy in a small group, life in a community of believers, support through close friends, and faithful models in people who have walked the journey ahead of them. No one finds healing alone. Healing comes in a threefold relationship: God, community, and ourselves.

Seek professional help. Most of all, ask for help! Somehow, we are conditioned to resist help. We won't ask for help; we won't seek help. This is particularly true when someone suggests we might need professional help such as therapy, a support group, or even weeks of intensive treatment. We resist. We think we can handle it. And we sometimes fail. God's grace comes through professional therapy as well as a believing community. They are not mutually exclusive. They are complementary.

Just as medicine heals the body, so therapy serves the emotional health of the mind and soul. Sometimes we need others to listen with an experienced ear because their wisdom hears what our tone-deafness cannot. We need others to speak into our lives in healing ways, help us reframe our experiences, and reorient our vision. Don't deny the grace God offers through these servants.

Worship with a community. I know all too well how difficult it can be to worship with a community of believers in the midst of grief. Some never return. It is especially hard when our assemblies are filled with high-energy praise and testimonies are filled with success stories. Rarely, it seems, do we find a place for lament within our assemblies.

Nevertheless, Jesus is there. The one who asked God, "Why have you forsaken me?" is the same one who, among his brothers and sisters, in the midst of the congregation, praised God (Psalm 22:1, 22; Hebrews 2:12). In communal worship, we stand in the assembly of believers and join the assembly around the throne. Through worship, we see the world rightly, and we experience the future, as well as the present, heavenly Jerusalem. Worship reorients us, comforts us, and encourages us.

As we close this study, I invite you to reflect on and discuss with those around you some final questions that can help you process your suffering, or perhaps that of others around you:

1. How does it make a difference to know that God is ultimately good and that God has our best interests at heart?
2. How has this study helped you to better endure loss? Will you be able to more effectively support others when they suffer?
3. Are you able or empowered to trust God now more than you could before you began this study? In what ways is this true, and where do you identify the need for further reflection or processing?

Additional Space for Journaling

John Mark Hicks
Teaches *Anchors for the Soul*

ANCHORS
for the SOUL
Video Course

A Video Course for Groups and Individuals

- Go Deeper into the Content of the Book
- Listen to Heart-Felt Stories from the Author
- Spark Discussions with Your Group

Get access at

HIMPUBLICATIONS.COM